T0131765

Heaven on Earth

Spiritual Healing in Ancestral Genetic Memory

Angel Manu

BALBOA.
PRESS
A DIVISION OF HAY HOUSE

Balboa Press books may be ordered through booksellers or by contacting:

Balboa Press
A Division of Hay House
1663 Liberty Drive
Bloomington, IN 47403
www.balboapress.com
1 (877) 407-4847

ISBN: 978-1-5043-3287-3 (sc)
ISBN: 978-1-5043-3286-6 (e)

Library of Congress Control Number: 2015907473

Print information available on the last page.

Balboa Press rev. date: 05/15/2015

About the Author

Angel Manu is a gifted spiritual medium, a Māori matakite. Her intuitive insights are presented as a free-flowing matrix of enlightened patterning. She compares the resonating spiritual messages to the shifting milky hues of the crystal Opalite. The veil is lifted briefly to reveal the flashing fiery amber underneath.

She lives in the sunny Bay of Plenty, performing genetic-cloud healings at local spiritual meetings, at fairs and markets, at health expos, and in the privacy of her home. She believes that in order to become an integrated soul, we each need to heal the trauma of our ancestral past.

Angel is from Ngāpuhi and Ngāti Pōrou, with Welsh, Irish, English, and French ancestry. She believes that people are a result of all the memories of their genetic cloud. If we can heal the hurts of our past, we can become wonderful, compassionate human beings living out heaven on earth.

To my daughter, Hazel, and my three granddaughters, Kate, Bella, and Scarlett

It was very real and unlike anything I've experienced before. It was like releasing the old DNA messages and acknowledging the new. For nearly a month before my healing, I was feeling old, with a lot of aching and throbbing in my muscles and bones. It was terrible. Coming to Angel Manu was like getting rid of the old way of being, and now I feel like a totally new person. I'm alive – really alive.
Sue (Tauranga) November 2014

Contents

Introduction

I am not actually sure when I performed my first genetic-cloud healing, but I know that I have been helping souls bound to earth for quite some time now. This particular process focuses on communication between the traumatized spirit, me as the medium, and the living relative present in the room. It is not a past-life regression but an ancestral regression. However, it is similar in that there is an emotional release of energy; this can be a bit startling, even for me.

A pattern of emotional behaviours and connections to health issues appears during the process. We create our earthbound reality, so our life paths are determined not only by our choices but also by the history in our genetic memory created by our ancestors. The story in our genetic clouds can never be predicted completely, so I am continuously astonished by the myriad ways people have died, especially when a murderous plan was afoot. This work is certainly gruesome but never boring. Nonetheless, I avoid overly violent and demonic movies. In fact, they scare me more than my work, which may surprise you after reading a few of these stories; you will probably wonder how I sleep at night.

The events related here include a mix of inspiring spiritual experiences. Some are about witchcraft, some are about spirit guardians, and others are about clearing earthbound spirits. I think all spiritual stories are intriguing, and it seems that a lot of cruelty happened during the Tribal Magical Era, and then later in the Religious Era with the evangelical crusades. There was a lot of superstition in the past, and religious-based judgements were responsible for the vicious deaths of many of our ancestors.

The requests I've received recently from murdered souls trying to show me where their body parts were disposed of are not shared in this book. It isn't my line of work. I have decided to leave those challenges to other experts and to firmly deflect that energy away from me. I don't enjoy terrified victims trying to wake me up in the middle of the night.

I hope that you will enjoy this journey and discover that there are earthbound ghosts in your genes.

First Integrated Insight

Fear, fear, fear: organized, genetic
Nightmare – primordial soup.
Integrate the steps. Have
Emotional results. Hey, you,
Out there in your fake, programmed tribal
Security! Hey, you, out there with your
Fake programmed egotistical impulse!
Hey, you, out there in your fake, programmed
Multiplex resolutions! Hey, you, out
There in your fake, programmed
Self-Success!
Hey, you, out there in your Moral
Stigma: Remove the evil brain into extinction –
Pineal extraction of
Magical thinking.

Now, sensitive me; the rain pours down
As I embrace it all. No fight, no more.

The Stone People and the Slaves

I had some very interesting experiences in the Nelson and Marlborough region of New Zealand when I worked with a great *tohunga*.[1] In my line of work, you accept all manner of strange phenomena, and after a while, you integrate them as a natural part of your journey.

There is an area where pre-European and pre-Māori people used to live. These ancient people used to cast spells to control the elements. One day, as we, the tohunga and me, walked up a fairly ordinary path in a wood in a fairly ordinary part of town, a rock called out to me.

My reaction was disbelief at first, just like most people would feel. I thought, "Did I really hear it? Ah … yes, I did." The plea of help came from a rock slightly bigger than a football. I had to listen for a while because the manner of a problem helps me bring the power of compassion to help out. An ancient person confided in me that he was a victim of an ancient spell. An angry and demented man had gone about, trapping the souls of tribal members into stones with his skills in witchcraft.

This angry person must have travelled to do his work because when we released the soul of the person who had asked for help, a hundred other souls were released too. They flew past us like a dark cloud of birds, singing their gratitude as they passed. There were some local inhabitants and many from the North Island. We were happy for them to be free to go to their spiritual home. It seems they were all related, and I believe that it was great for them to be together again. As their souls returned to the sky, I sensed a massive release of energy. I felt electrified for days afterward.

Our forefathers are always with us. We are connected to their memories.
The cruel intentions of others cause their souls distress.

---

[1]   Tohunga: Wizard, priest

Because of a feudal system in place, slaves tend the gardens that are essential for the survival of the group that controls the area. I'm uninterested in dealing with the perpetrators of an injustice. I prefer to bring love to the people suffering at the hands of such controlling practices.

In the distance, we could see the ghosts of *waka*[2] in the estuary. They were very busy, patrolling the waterways. They didn't see us because we were in another time dimension. However, the slaves saw us.

A child of about twelve hid behind a tree for quite some time, staring at me. I assumed an expression that I hoped would convey, "It's okay; I'm not going to hurt you." I sat at the picnic table nearby, pretending to ignore him. Soon, he had enough courage to walk across the clearing to communicate with me. I learnt that he was the leader of a group of children. The waterways and the patrolling boats kept them from escaping. They had been brought to the island as working slaves and traded in exchange for food. He told me that every day, they were taken across the estuary and made to dig trenches and scrape rocks in the huge gardens.

The most moving part of my encounter with this boy was that he wanted me to free the souls of the children who couldn't leave because they had been eaten. I suppose that the owners saw cannibalism as a perfectly natural right. However, I was intrigued to learn that the affected souls were trapped.

They all came out of the thicket when their leader confirmed his friendship with us. They ran to me as if I were their mother, and my tears fell. We told them that there was a better place for them to go in spirit. The tohunga began the incantations to send them to the light, where they would be safe.

They were all insistent that their leader go with them to this new place too. He was torn between agreeing and staying to take care of the land, but when an angel appeared, he didn't waste any time at all! Whoosh, he was off! They all flew away together, and their happiness left a trail of giggles that hung in the air for quite some time. It was one of the most moving releases of souls I have witnessed. The trauma of innocent children always opens my heart.

The tohunga I was paired with on that trip will stay anonymous here because I respect and guard her *mana*.[3] I remain very grateful to her for choosing my *matakite*[4] skills to see and communicate with the unseen. I regard my work with her as truly inspiring. It was the motivation for many future clearings and healings of traumatized souls.

---

[2]   Waka: Canoe
[3]   Mana: Psychic force
[4]   Matakite: Seer

Second Integrated Insight

Yo!
Ho! Hello!
So, bro. Go! Yo!
Solar-system flight.
Stumble duality into the
Night. Every day, broken
Perfect. Night. Experience
Of life. Treaty no more. Sure.
Sins in graciousness. Ignorant.
Be in the primordial soup. Ho! Yo!
Seconds perfect. Jump now! Jump now!
Minutes. Ho! Yo! Jump now! Jump now! Ho!
Hours passed. Don't let the fast last. Transcend hours past.
Honour. Who? Not me! Not you! Ho! Yo! Jump into what's right.

Ding!

Kaitiaki Spirit Guardian

The story of one of my guardian spirits starts with a spiritual journey to an area on the East Coast of New Zealand. I had been pulled to the island on several occasions. On this particular occasion, I visited a wise woman from England who helped me release a domineering past-life experience. She was very hospitable and gracious. However, she and her husband had been struggling to live comfortably in this valley for quite some time because there was strife amongst the neighbours.

I offered to walk the land to see if there were any unsettled spirits. I knew that further south, a surprise attack from the mainland had occurred a few centuries beforehand. Wherever blood is spilt, genetic memory in the land will reveal the history. I only found one memory of death in a small ravine from an attack on a person, whom I then released into the light. My host took me further up the valley to a knoll that looked down on the scattering of farmhouses below. I wandered around for a short time, and then a large *kaitiaki*[5] swooped down and stood towering above me. He was furious.

I was definitely alarmed. He was a formidable and fierce lizard-looking creature. As I stood my ground, he turned around and tried to defecate on us. I moved quickly, guarding my companion. However, I sensed that the guardian's anger was more to do with his pride and frustration, rather than being aimed at me personally.

You will always find emotional reasons behind psychic disturbances.

Carefully and bravely, I asked for the reason behind his discontent. He told us that he had been living there in spirit peacefully for 50,000 years after the Ice Age, until foreign settlers came. They disregarded his rights to ownership of the valley. In fact, they not only ignored his presence but also defecated throughout the valley, defiling his holy home. Dragons are archaic creatures,

---

5   Kaitiaki: Guardian, minder, keeper

so they have very grounded reasons for their feelings. Therefore, always be wary and respectful of their territorial instincts.

I immediately thought that this kaitiaki had been insulted out of ignorance. I explained the predicament to the landowner, who was very concerned with the revelation and its implications. The kaitiaki grew quieter. After some thought, I requested that a human sign be erected so that anyone entering the valley would know that it was his, and people would thereby respect his ancient ownership. The local wise woman thought this was a fair request. She also agreed to share this sacred knowledge with her neighbours so that they would think differently about their land and its future use.

However, our work wasn't finished yet. The kaitiaki unexpectedly challenged me to stay under his mastery. Naturally, I refused, insisting that it would be foolish to stay. I explained that the human gift from God was my spiritual free will. He sulked like a disappointed puppy, and I realized the simplicity of his nature.

A month or so later, I was driving through the Waikato on my journey to Nelson in the South Island, when a whooping noise above my car gave me a fright. The kaitiaki appeared, swooping above and in front of me, avoiding the poles on the side of the motorway with great skill. He declared his devotion to me as a protector for life, especially during travel. His presence makes a clear path on the road where angry spirits and other ancient *taniwha*[6] reside. I am eternally grateful for his gift of love.

---

[6]   Taniwha: A formidable sacred creature

Third Integrated Insight

—⁓∘◦⟞◦◉◦⟝∘◦⁓—

What I observe is wave-like. I pass through the concrete world. I'm jumping a photon wave.

I pass through and then come into connection with the phenomenon that is entangling me.

Your unfortunate life, your conditions preset – transformation
of thoughts into negative events in life.

Some people die. Some people live. You escape from nothing,
suffering guaranteed. No special selection or protection.

Entangled with the negative. Attached at the other end. My fortunate life, my
conditions preset – transformation of thoughts into positive events in life.

I will change you.

3

Tahitian Ancestor

My story now takes us to Tahiti. This amazing genetic healing involves, yet again, spells and witchcraft from the Tribal Magic Era. Tribal members synchronize their behaviour because individualism can destroy the fabric of the group. Furthermore, the mana and power of the collective is weakened by individual defiance. In this story, I share the defiance and consequent dilemma of a patron's ancestors. We will call the child Teiki for the sake of this shared healing experience. Teiki was a spoilt boy, doted on by his mother, Maeva. He was prone to getting his way.

On this particular occasion, Teiki wanted to go fishing on the reef that provided most of the food for the tribe. However, he could not go unless his older brother, Meimana, went with him. This was a rule. Meimana had to provide the protection incantations and stay on the *va'a*[7] to help retrieve the fishing catch and to help Teiki back aboard.

On this particular day, Meimana had other plans. He had promised to be with the girl he loved. So, naturally, he refused Teika's request for accompaniment. Maeva insisted that the older brother go, and as he must obey his mother without question, he reluctantly accompanied his sibling. Meimana was angry with his brother. His mother's preference for Teika made him furiously jealous. As they paddled to the reef, Meimana's negative thoughts grew and grew until he wished Teika dead. The weeds heard his negative prayers, so when Teika was swimming around the bottom of the reef, they grabbed him tightly and held him there. Teika wanted to return to the va'a, but Meimana ignored him. The water was very clear, so Meimana could see the expression on his drowning brother's face as he struggled to death. At last, he had more power than his brother.

This betrayal was excruciating for Teika. My patron wept and explained that his family still suffered much from betrayal. I spoke to Teika and told him that his suffering was being acknowledged by his living relative. As a nine-year-old boy in spirit, he was not shaken by this concept or by our

---

7   Va'a: canoe

presence. He welcomed the chance to talk about his feelings. He also knew that my intentions were born of compassion for his continued suffering which had stayed in the genetic memory of the family, preventing him from leaving. Together, I guided both relatives to discuss the pain that each had suffered. I guided my patron to send loving feelings to the child to heal the grave injustice of his death and to offer a release into the light. An angel arrived, and they left. The departure seemed very welcome. Teiki had received love and understanding from a living relative, so he was ready to leave earth.

Fourth Integrated Insight

———ᴡᴏᴏᴇᴛᴏᴏᴛᴏᴏᴡ———

In the spaces of the wave, we can create peace and beauty;
Or with the mind, a destructive bomb!

Dichroic soul, in Opalite, shine. Existence is also evident. Aware of me,
synchronized. Two parts of self, created. Anticipated dichroic light being.
Internal world, pathway to knowing. Manifestation of our creation. Hello, hell
on earth. Learn the rules pretty quickly. Conform to the preset conditions.

Control doll. I'm not sacrificed. I'm not the lamb. I'm not deluded or dreaming,
either. Cling to your righteous viewpoints as you fall of the cliff.

Entropy! Entropy! Disordered disease. You spend a lot of time reordering
yourself, don't you? Okay, I have no influence. I let it go! I'll try
expanding your equal probabilities. No … I'm outta here.

Womb of warm liquid. Control doll. Go away!

Now, what do I really want to create in this world again?

Intentions and Manipulations

When you intend to manifest something in this world, you will manipulate your environment to get it. We often get what we think we need by conforming to the systems that have already been set up. If the systems are too difficult or if some people create more than their share because the system works better for them, you will learn a dualistic reality of this earth: there are rich people, and there are poor people.

Our anxieties build as someone or something challenges our intentions to be rich. Therefore, we often use our power to control and manipulate others to get wealth. This is evident in today's society as the need to succeed often overwhelms the needs of the heart.

I have free will to support the process I deem will benefit my needs. However, may God give me the courage to make decisions that come from the heart, for this is truly spiritual.

Fifth Integrated Insight

―――⁓∾◦⎯⦥◦⎯⦣◦⎯⦥◦⎯∾⁓―――

Be quiet. Observe.
Spirit of existence
See the truth;
Be freed.
Bondage belief,
Bondage attachments,
Bondage ideas –
Minds giving the meanings.

Memorize, imagine, analyse.
Reconfigure insights, experiences.
You desire. Concretize. Label everything you see.
Natural response:
Automated behaviour.
Genetic memory perceives threats today.
The outer experience,
The meanings,
Upset your ideas.
I'm threatening.

Profound perceptions –
Develop, develop, develop.
Profound deceptions –
Develop, develop, develop.
Concretize beliefs. Align with your friends. Challenge the family.
Challenge the community. Something doesn't feel right.

The Murdered Pacifist

My next story of a genetic-memory healing comes from a young man who worked with me in the field of understanding the right- and left-brain dualities. He was predominantly right-brained, so he struggled to accommodate the dominating patterns of left-brained, logical-thinking personalities in his environment. He had never considered that his thinking processes were very different to most other modern thinkers, so when he tried to fit into the system, he felt unwell.

We developed strategies that gave him free will and the right to be who he really was – a predominantly right-brained psychic healer. It wasn't surprising that his ancestral story stretched back to a civil war. I connected to his earthbound ancestor, whom I will call Mac, on the battlefield. Mac was a soldier of fortune but also a pacifist and a Scotsman. I discovered that it wasn't the enemy who had murdered him; it was his comrades-in-arms. They saw him as a traitor because he avoided using his gun and refused to kill anyone.

He was a gentle, cheerful person who liked to play music and sing. The other soldiers enjoyed the benefits of his musical talents, but after a while, they were tired of the self-important dreams that he talked about far too often for their comfort. He repeatedly spoke about his intentions to love and provide for his new bride, who was waiting for his return. He couldn't stop talking about the cottage of his imagination on the reward land the soldiers had been promised for fighting in the gruesome war. After a few skirmishes, however, when Mac failed to protect his fellow soldiers and survived by avoiding a fight most of the time, his comrades plotted to finish him off. They also laid claim to his land through using his official papers. Identity theft is not merely a contemporary phenomenon.

As Mac was sitting on a log beside his tent, one of his comrades crept up behind him and garrotted him. Together, the soldiers wrapped Mac's dead body in his tent and buried him. No one discovered what had taken place. They believed that he was a coward, and therefore he had received his just desserts.

Mac's wife was left wondering as to his whereabouts, and she assumed that he had changed his mind or hadn't been able to return. She died after many years of waiting for his return, still fretting. Mac knew of her plight and stayed earthbound because he felt betrayed and bereft.

This event had all the elements of traumatic death – betrayal and abandonment. My client related the isolation and mistrust he felt around groups of men, and speaking his truth often gave him trouble. This connects to the garrotting in the past to keep Mac quiet.

We spoke to Mac about his despair and grief. We processed his traumatized feelings by listening to his story and sharing our feelings of compassion and love for him. My student was brilliant at acknowledging how Mac's tragedy had affected his relationships and how his personal difficulties seemed to mirror Mac's personality.

Amazingly, Mac's wife appeared in spirit, and they were reunited at long last. They left for heaven together. They were strong believers in Christianity, so their marriage vows were for life. I was not at all surprised with their destination of the afterlife of their beliefs.

> *He stood tall like a kahikatea,[8] peering between the leaves for his heaven on earth.*
> *"Help me to help you so I can help all of us," he declared.*
> *The forest heard his profound intention.*
> *And so, it was manifest.*

Testimonial

Everyone has always said to me "You're always in your head." And all I could ever think was "Well yeah, but what else can I do?" This amazing genetic-cloud Healing provided me with the tools I needed to actually be the person I wanted to be in this lifetime. Working with this matakite challenged me to change my ways, think differently about life and most importantly trust myself to be who I always knew I could be.

There is much more to this world than I could have ever realized, and I feel privileged that I can now experience it in all its beauty and power. I was searching for an answer to why life has never felt quite right, and in her, I found it. She supported me through everything, teaching me all I needed to know, and set me on a self-supported path to take on my own life. I now feel free to change it however I want.

(Scott)

---

8   Kahikatea: a tall endemic tree in New Zealand

Sixth Integrated Insight

Nailed to a grand cross.
Sun in Aquarius. Valued independence.
Humanitarian activist. Save our souls.
Ascendant and Moon in Taurus rising.
Physical security – material, steady, affectionate.
Drive, will, and initiative.

Mars near Moon. Hello, Aggressive Mother.
Father's strong influence –
Parents lovingly at war.

I know heaven on earth. Release the ambition.
Valuable associations. Real commitment.
Feelings of security must take a mental form.

Venus opposite Uranus. Neptune opposite Mars.
Friendly philosophy. Deception and fraud.
Stick it out, no matter how difficult.
Fixed, fixed, fixed.

Saturn in Sagittarius, mutable philosophy.
Jupiter in Libra – optimism. Try again.

Spiritual revolution,
Hung on a grand cross.

6

Family Cruelty

The cruelty inflicted by family members to shut someone up or to manipulate their possessions is very interesting. One particular genetic-cloud healing was fascinating in that a very elderly man took so long to die that the family nailed his coffin closed as soon as they convinced themselves that he had stopped breathing. He woke up from narcolepsy to die of suffocation and rejection. The present-day relative had very difficult breathing issues, and the bereaved ancestor wouldn't cooperate easily, as his hurt was so profound.

Another earthbound victim was Teiki's brother, Heimana. When the elders of the tribe realized that Heimana had used his negative thoughts to kill his brother, they placed him in a circle of stones. A *ta'hua*[9] cast a spell on the circle, which forbade the young man from leaving the enclosed area. He suffered terribly from starvation as punishment. His mother, Maeva, was forced to watch his death because the tribal leaders deemed that she made a decision that the tribe could no longer fish in that area of the reef. The agony shared in that family's genetic memory was excruciating, to say the least.

I am so grateful to be able to help children who have been lost, injured, and unable to call for help. One day, a child approached me while I was taking a stroll in a wetlands park. He was suffering terribly from dying in a car accident. He was disoriented and couldn't find his mother. When I explained that he was a spirit, he didn't know what to do next, as he had never been taught about heaven or angels. In contrast, when you have a plan regarding death, your spirit will automatically take you to the place you believe you will go. This is why I warn people who blatantly and jokingly announce that they will probably go to hell. In this case, the boy's mother had been an atheist, so he had no philosophy of God or baptism. His love for his mother had kept him earthbound in search of her, and she was nowhere! I took the initiative and called an angel, with whom the child happily ascended to heaven.

---

[9]   Ta'hua: witch doctor

Animals can stay around in spirit too. I have helped disgruntled bulls. Cats often stay on the owner's property for some time, zooming around as if they weren't dead, and then they either return to the earth essence or stay to keep their owner company. It is not uncommon for a cheerful small dog to appear to me out of the blue, asking that I pass on a message to an owner who happens to be near me. The owners often listen because they usually have a positive synchronized relationship and memory of the animal in their genetic-clouds. Horses are extremely loyal, especially war and police horses.

Seventh Integrated Insight

—~~∿∽⟋⟍⟋⟍∽∿~~—

Emotional injustice
To co-create.
Release the sin before
The conscious alteration,
The perpetrated aberration,
Lessening the life force of the intelligent creator.

It was very real.
The old DNA messages
Acknowledge the new,
But feel old,
Aching and throbbing,
Muscles and bones.

Terrible life.
Get rid of the old way –
Totally new and alive today!
I survived –
Phew!
Relief and exemplary healing.

Good job!

Relationships in Past Lives

I have observed a similar spiritual healing process attached to traumatized memories in genetic-cloud healings as in past-life experiences. They both involve the presence of an observer and the emotion of compassion. However, my past-life experiences are usually connected to a specific person in my current reality.

My first past-life experience takes us to India. I was married to a wealthy elderly man, and I was only sixteen or seventeen years old. He was a gentle person of sixty years; even though he was elderly, I loved him dearly. As you can imagine, I valued being an attractive and lively person. I had many expectations. Unfortunately, he died suddenly, and as was the custom there, I was burnt alive on a pyre with him. It was extremely painful, and the promise that I would stay with him in spirit was never fulfilled until I met him again as a lover, quite a few centuries later. I will call this second man Don for the sake of this story. He was around ten years older than me. Don was a New Zealander and a spiritual person with a gentle nature. One evening when we were in the middle of lovemaking, my feelings were so profound that the past-life experience recalled here was triggered. I couldn't stop crying and was totally beside myself. I told him about my feelings of abandonment and the extreme cruelty I had suffered.

Don empathized with me. As if he were my elderly husband from that past life, he kindly explained that if I hadn't been sacrificed with him, I would have been abandoned and unable to take care of myself. Worse yet, another man would have claimed me, and my life may have been Hell. It was very helpful for me to understand this. Don offered compassion, which helped to heal my broken heart. I still don't like this ceremony of wives being cremated with their husbands, but I now see it from a different perspective and can let go of the crippling judgement. He admitted that he should have explained this ceremony at the time of marriage, but he was selfish and was afraid of losing me. He had expected himself to live longer than he actually did. Don caressed my body and soothed me with his soft whispers until I feel asleep in his arms, a happy young girl once again.

I experienced another past-life story about a man. He was in a female form as my grandmother sometime during the eighteenth century, living somewhere in northern England. She was ill for quite some time and lived far away from where I worked for a lord in western England. I remember taking the long journey by horse, which required many days of galloping to reach her. She died before I (as this man) reached her on one of these journeys, and she never forgave me for this. Of course, it was impracticable for me to be with her in time on this occasion. Strangely, I never felt that I could do enough to please this person, so we departed each other. When I left, I felt that the debt had been paid, as I had supported him diligently for several years. I think my own sense of fairness settled the equation of energy.

Eighth Integrated Insight

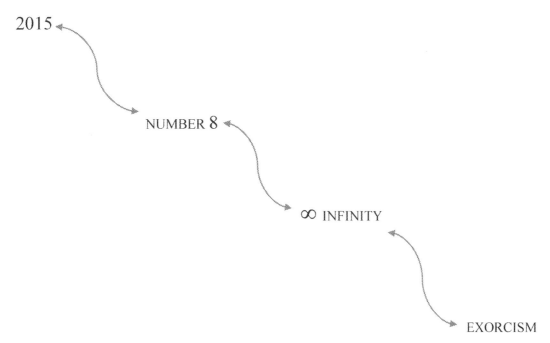

2015

NUMBER 8

∞ INFINITY

EXORCISM

Black Witch

Being wary of black witches is good advice. They will enslave men and women through sensual bondage, sheer malice, and a desire to own you. The greatest gift from light is your free will. You are your own person. A black witch knows that you like to empower yourself through your own decisions, so she will manipulate your desires and increase them until you are a slave to them. She understands perfectly how to expand your needs. By pretending to be your best friend through flattery and good times and by supplying you with everything your needy mind desires, she will control you.

We are all curious and have all fallen prey to the calculations of others. I want to share a story here which demonstrates that you can foil a black witch's plans. However, it might involve an exorcism and the police.

This story is story is set in the 1980s in Wellington. The couple to which this happened, whom I will call Alan and Liz, were adventurous and young. They both had jobs and a good cash flow, and they loved sex. They were party animals who were vain about their bodies and possessions. Scuba diving, water skiing, and eating extravagant dinners were high on the entertainment list for Alan and Liz.

Businesses thrived because there was a hefty entertainment tax incentive encouraging a lot of drinking and late lunches. Pornography and pot were available at sophisticated parties. Swinging was definitely an option too.

Liz was ten years younger than Alan and a little naïve about his enthusiasm for sex. She was more interested in pumping up his happiness than her own, but she drew a line at swinging. So, when they met Amelia and Sid through a photography party, Alan made arrangements with Amelia and Sid behind Liz's back to feed his ever-increasing sexual appetite.

You see, whatever you focus on will grow. So, if you are surrounded by sensual photography, flirtatious people, sensual music, and alcohol, you are in line for an extra naughty time involving pot and pornography that probably culminates in an orgy. However, Liz never went for the extra naughty. She preferred to get boozed and then take her man home for sex.

When Liz discovered that Amelia and Sid were producing pornographic movies, she reported it to the authorities. She was astonished to discover that there was already a dossier on the couple, but the police department was waiting for an official complaint. Liz felt sick that she had associated with people whose morals were outside her own boundaries. She enjoyed having fun, but this was definitely outside her comfort zone, and she was a Christian of sorts.

That evening, Alan and Liz discussed the events over a drink in a bar. Alan said he supported Liz's action, so she thought that they had narrowly escaped being implicated. Of course, she had no idea that Alan was fully engaged with the perverted couple's activities. Alan immediately started behaving paranoid. He spotted two men in the bar, watching them. Liz had no idea who they were, but Alan must have known them, as he wanted to leave immediately.

As the couple drove home, Alan became panicky and started driving erratically. He was convinced that they were being followed. Liz felt uneasy about his strange reaction. When they arrived at the house, he started speaking gibberish and talking to a hairbrush. And then he raped Liz. Liz heard a clear voice say that she needed to get help from a minister immediately. It was as if her guardian angel woke her up to something more sinister than she could have imagined. Liz also had a strange vision that twenty men were having sex with Amelia. It seemed real and violent.

Liz instinctively drew crosses on twenty pieces of paper and stuck them on the walls. She rang a local minister, and he listened carefully to the unfolding story. He came immediately and prayed with Liz until daylight. Exhausted, she slept most of the day. The minister said he would come back and collect both Liz and her husband around five that evening and take them to a special service. Alan was sitting blankly at this stage, mumbling gibberish. It appeared that he had gone quite mad.

That evening, the minister explained that there would be a hands-on cleansing and some chanting. The meeting place was underneath a stone building. When Liz went to look for it at a later date, she couldn't find the building at all. It was very mysterious. There were at least fifty people there, all dressed in white. There were many candles and a lot of chanting. Alan shook and convulsed as the devotees laid their hands on him. Liz wept because she realized how much she had strayed from the path she meant to follow. The negative energy was released from both Liz and Alan, and they were healed.

The next day, Liz developed flu-like symptoms, so she went to a local doctor. She requested a remedy and some time off work. The doctor asked her to hold out her hands. It was a peculiar request, but she understood as soon as he looked in her eyes and asked, "Have you been playing with witchcraft?" Shocked that he should know her plight so clearly, she broke down. The doctor had worked in Africa and knew the symptoms well. He explained that occult spells were generally limited to about thirty kilometres, so he advised her to leave town immediately. He also warned her to watch out for occult movements in the future.

As Liz walked home, she came across Amelia and Sid's receptionist, who was walking around in a daze, smoking heavily. Liz kept her distance, but when the woman saw Liz, she cried out, "Oh my God, they have gone! There is nothing in the office. It is empty!" Liz briefly explained what had happened to her and Alan. A weird smile appeared on the woman's face as she declared, "Didn't you know that Amelia is a black witch?"

Liz was quick to leave the area, and she never associated with anyone who remotely reminded her of Amelia or Sid. Seductive charms and black magic rituals never interested her again. Alan, however, never recovered.

Ninth Integrated Insight

Mind of relativity,
Entropy, centropy, yin and yang of earth.
Minds – productive, naturally disordered.
Less energy, satisfaction diminished.

If I have a choice,
Keep my life organized.
Use more energy and a lot more effort.
Meet the needs of others.
Expectations, beliefs, requirements,
In order to succeed expend a lot of energy.

I am clear. I want to create,
Devoid of controlling energy fields.
It's my life process, a whole lot smoother
At a micro level, not a macro level.

The forces of duality do not affect me now.
I am a remote viewer.
I am one person living in two realities.
Nobody notices me
In the wave of creation.

Elven Guardian

This is another story of a guardian spirit. Alice and I met at a spiritual gathering where I was reading tarot and performing genetic-cloud healings. She was touring New Zealand at the time and had just been to a summer solstice gathering near Wellington, where there is a replica of Stonehenge.

She was very enthusiastic about my work because she had been a research scientist before her conversion to astrology. My psychic work in epigenetic memory and my unique symbolism in tarot intrigued her immensely. Very quickly, we connected with her ancestral home. I have a Welsh connection on my mother's side through early New Zealand settlers. Because of this, I was able to share the magical thinking of my childhood about toadstools and faerie in the garden.

I tuned into this woman's genetic-cloud memory fairly quickly. Her traumatized earthbound ancestor had been locked away in a small straw shed attached to the main house for many years. The large house had white walls made of stone. It became obvious that this rather timid person was a hermaphrodite, so I assumed that hiding at the back of the property was relevant to the duality of her sexual organs. However, as the ancestor became more comfortable with us, she sat on my knee to listen to our discussions around famous homes and castles.

Now, I know that the Welsh can be tiny because my great-grandmother had to jump into her seat, as her legs were short. We always laughed when we visited her – she had a lot of gaiety about her.

However, as Alice's ancestor became more relaxed, I noticed pointy ears and patches of soft black fur on her body. She had large, mesmerising dark-blue eyes. I was so glad that Alice knew immediately that it was an elven creature.

The elf started shaking as I listened to her gruesome story. She was regarded as a magical and special creature, and although the relatives who lived in the house fed her regularly, they found her a burden. In addition, they wouldn't kill her because of their magical thinking. To kill an elf would bring disaster.

It appears that the elven creature had lived there for a very long time. She was named Elwydden, and she didn't know if she was the last elf to be alive. She couldn't remember when she had seen another person like herself. This was circa 1560, rather late for a mythical creature like this to appear, so I expect that her protection had worked for some time.

Poor Elwydden was betrayed by someone in the village who probably wanted a reward. Mythical creatures were still being culled because the fear of tribal ideology was still strong in the area at that time. Armour-clad soldiers associated with church authority came and dragged her into the open, where she was hacked to pieces.

Recalling this horrible death made Elwydden tremble. We began healing her traumatized death by acknowledging her cruel isolation and execution. Alice was particularly distressed by the cruelty. We both wept compassionate tears for the elf. This emotional empathy started a healing in Alice's memory. She recalled that her father had been abandoned and sent back to his birth home when he was only three years old. It was a perfect match in genetic-cloud memory. Alice felt a release which healed her immediately.

However, we weren't done yet. I was curious as to why the elf had appeared, and I was at a loss regarding what to do next. I had no idea where her spiritual home would be, apart from where she had been born and killed. Elwydden understood immediately and leapt from my arms to her descendant's arms. She didn't want to go anywhere; she wanted to be Alice's spirit guardian.

Alice was totally delighted, and I knew that they would take good care of each other. Like my spirit guardian dragon from Aotearoa, this elf had chosen Alice as her special friend – for life. What a lucky lady from Powys!

Tenth Integrated Insight

———∿∘ᴏᴇᴛᴏᴏᴇᴛᴏ∘∿———

Genetic memory.
Magical thinkers,
The gift of knowing.

Existence of angels,
Spirit guardians,
Communication with the dead.

Accepting,
Liberating,
Without even trying.
A process of knowing
They are there, setting you apart.

Speak to Jesus of Nazareth
Every day as my friend,
My brother and friend in spirit.

Ancestors who
Experienced an injustice:
Do take them seriously.
You can create heaven on earth by reconciling the sins of your fathers.
Your genetic cloud is like the Book of Life.
You will raise the dead and heal them.

Revenge of the Wise Woman

The crossroads of Christianity and witchcraft often arise in this work. It seems that the worst of both conscious states emerges, so the power struggle is often peppered with cruelty.

This genetic-cloud healing story presents a king. We will call him John. His living relative, we will call Margaret. As soon as she arrived, the hairs on my arms stood on end. I knew we were in for an interesting journey. I don't experience many connections with kings because most people are not related to royalty. King John was eviscerated, and his entrails were stuffed down his throat. His sword was plunged down the back of his neck, and his toenails were pulled out.

Apparently, John was arrogant and proud. He had ordered all the natural healers and wise women to be tortured. This was during a time when Christians persecuted pagans, especially those who were into witchcraft. In this instance, the enforcers had extracted a particular wise woman's toenails and broken her ankles so that she couldn't bring people remedies. The locals were furious. She was highly respected and loved, so the common folk took their revenge by imposing the same cruelties and torture back on their ruler. Actually, they gave this wise woman the honour of pulling out his toenails. She stored them in a jar and cast a spell on it so that he couldn't leave the earth.

Therefore, I needed to persuade the wise woman to release the spell. It was like a movie. We begged her to forgive him. She must have been a reasonable sort of person because she whacked his sword on the ground. It emitted a blue ray of light, and the jar of nails broke open. The spell was undone. She disappeared quickly.

One good thing that came from this was John's repentance for being arrogant and cruel. He had learnt what it was like to be on the receiving end of torture. We forgave him, and he was released to the spiritual home of his choice, heaven.

We were humbled by the process, and Margaret's outcome was that she could see that arrogance and pride had caused huge rifts in her family. She took the opportunity to soften her heart and felt a release of healing.

Eleventh Integrated Insight

Coyote – fenced offence.
Dragging her down, I see. I see.
Stop! Different now.
The monarch butterfly,
Fascinating wing discovery.
Numerical coding, unique.
Fostering the love – operate, operate.
Extract the hurt wing.
Done!
Grateful love, exchange numerical coding.
Jump, jump, jump. Numerical coding.
Dump, dump, dump. Coyote –
Gone!

Yes!

Be gone!

Spirits in Machinery and UFOs

Even with my extraordinary perceptions, I was in awe of the orange orb of light I saw over the *pā*.[10] A UFO expert explained that most of us try to disprove what we have seen and we even go into denial, but we often end up at the same place: we have to declare that we have seen a UFO.

After I saw a UFO, I had six months of spiritual unrest. I wrote about it, told everyone about it, researched previous sightings in the area, and had to conclude that the experience had a profound effect on me. My ancestor *Rangatira*[11] Patuone Maihe had a similar experience. He was a boy when the first foreign ship with white sails arrived in New Zealand. His awe was so profound; he had huge respect for the technical knowledge of the British.

It was a spiritual experience that urged him to be open to new and inspiring possibilities. He was known as the Peacemaker and is buried in a cemetery at the foot of Mt Victoria in Auckland. I respect this man for his valiant efforts to co-create a wholesome integrated community with the British. However, as a great tohunga said to me once, "Our treaty with God is balanced, but our treaties with men are always broken." Will treaties with aliens also be broken? I expect so because we always break our agreements and try to manipulate new ones to line the pockets of a few. That's the way it is.

My first experience of machinery having spirit was during a profound past-life regression. I was an intelligent spacecraft designed to collect floating debris. How can a piece of machinery be conscious? We already have robots that respond to light and sound independently of human instruction. And there are the fascinating concepts of cybernetics and the world functioning as a global brain. Machinery and technology are not separate from us, but part of us. We are creating a larger version of ourselves. In light of this, the probability of a conscious space-rubbish collector

---

10   Pā: Fortified tribal settlement
11   Rangitira: Chief

isn't too bizarre. However, I was aware of a dreadful sense of loneliness – lasting for eons! Rocks and mountains have a life force and feelings. Machinery is made from the earth, and we come from the Earth. So, from my perspective as an integrated soul, I choose to be respectful of all machinery, even a vacuum cleaner.

Twelfth Integrated Insight

I am the Copernicus of my salvation
And the Einstein of my creation.
Without earth, there would be no angels because our consciousness creates them.

No people,
No angels,
No meaning deep inside.

No torchlights to speak to the dead at night,
And no life to love or to hate.
Realize the truth before you die.

12

Angels and Ancestral Guides

I suppose a lot of people find it difficult to understand that Jesus cancelled the moral debt we have accumulated. Even though we have run out of moral credit after eons of evolutionary debauchery and evil, we have been forgiven. How does it work? We have all been traumatized by the destructive will of someone else's behaviour, and it is difficult for us to forgive them. In addition, the idea of confession and remorse to balance the books doesn't convince many hurt souls. So, we not only carry the emotional injury in our genetic memory to pass it on to our grandchildren but also choose to become earthbound traumatized spirits.

In light of this, I want to emphasize the extent to which our angels are here, helping us to move on and to forgive. They talk to us all the time and encourage us to become wise. They also whisper that we should forgive and let go for our own spiritual well-being and the well-being of our genetic evolution, to become integrated souls. Revenge and *utu*[12] serve only to recycle pain. Instead, we have to master our impulses to fight back when we are being threatened – turn the other cheek.

In this particular genetic-cloud healing, I learnt a new lesson. I usually work with women, so when a man requested a healing, I was a little surprised. However, I remembered that he had mentioned a health issue in his past that caused him continuous grief, and I trusted that all would be well. I also have an astounding track record of good outcomes. Sometimes I get challenged and a spirit won't come in, so I trust that I am not meant to heal the person at this specific time and place. If you are not getting a response, it is best to leave things as they are rather than forcing it.

So, this man arrived; I shall call him Steven. He was generally well-mannered and well-dressed. A little voice had warned me about him, but I thought he was just having a bad day. The session started fairly normally, and I explained – perhaps more thoroughly than usual – about how my process works and how he would be part of the healing triangle.

---

[12] Utu: Payback

A timid little girl was hanging in the periphery of my consciousness in spirit. I spotted her and allowed her time to come forward. It took a good ten minutes before she presented herself. I interpreted her caution as a need to trust me. Soon her story came. She had to take care of her sick grandfather, and she was only three or four years old. This was in feudal times, during which you had to pay the lord of the county 10 per cent of your harvest. This farmer had been too sick to till the soil, plant seeds, or even harvest that year. Usually, the community or your family would help. However, for this unfortunate man, his daughter went away to find a new life somewhere else after giving birth to her child. We will call the child Eve.

Calamity can strike at any moment. Eve's grandfather loved her so much, and he was determined to get better, but the lord was cruel and unforgiving. He offered the ailing man the following deal: "Let my paedophile son have his way with Eve, or hand her over permanently to work in my kitchen." The grandfather was in a terrible bind. These were the debauched conditions of this situation, and we cannot judge. Reluctantly, he allowed his grandchild to be raped. It was excruciating for him to hear her screams. She died as a result of the harm, and the grandfather died of a broken heart. He gave up the will to live.

So, there were two earthbound ancestors in Steven's genetic memory. He had to be healed from the awful emotions of being powerless over someone else's destructive will and from witnessing cruelty. I didn't spot at the moment that Steven wasn't very moved about the incident; he became mechanical. I released the ancestors to the light. They were happy that I had heard their story. Off they went, together.

I still couldn't understand the purpose of Steven coming. I sent him out the door as soon as possible. It took me six hours to really hear my spirit guardian. She agreed that it was great to release the ancestral victims, but I didn't pick up on Steven's motive.

She explained that he was the type who manipulates his presence into women's lives to take power over them. I was shocked. Of course, Eve tried to warn me from the beginning with her shyness.

I learnt a new lesson: the memory of sexual abuse transfers to genetic memory. Unfortunately for Steven, he was locked into a pattern of unhealthy relationships with women. Thank goodness for my spirit guardian's message. I am eternally grateful to the angels who bring us messages of wisdom and understanding.

Final Integrated Insight

Evil cosmic energy – dark.
Into many particles, we depart.
Burned by the sun and frozen by the ice –
The vacuum of space.
Compassion no more.

Self-conscious Sun,
Wobble no longer with your earthly attachment.
The fragments attach to Jupiter's cold shoulder.
New Moons appear in the giant spin.
Compassion no more.

Stray away and gather mass.
Rogue Moons, no star you will marry.
The curves of light,
No lens to watch
Ours and ours only:
The great misadventure,
Heaven on Earth

13

The Integrated Soul

You have been on the path of spiritual evolution recorded in your genetic memory. You have evolved spiritually through the eons, in this dualistic world, to learn about the choice to be an integrated soul. Your ancestors have often died tragic deaths as a result of cruelty, abandonment, and betrayal. Rather than focussing on the destructive will of those who harmed your ancestor, it is better to focus on your ancestor's pain and unhappiness. Your compassion and understanding release pain, an energy that does not serve you. When your ancestor's emotional pain has been healed, you too will be healed. You break the cycle of trauma in your genetic memory and feel liberated. The patterns of resentment, distrust, manipulation, loss, and helplessness in your family history will evaporate, along with symptoms like a dislocated neck, restricted breathing, aches and pains in limbs and fingers, continuous falls, mental disorientation, and many more health challenges.

I'm not claiming that genetic-cloud therapy will create heaven on earth for everyone, but I know a lot of people who have been inspired and changed by the process. Perhaps one day soon, we won't need a matakite medium like me to heal the trauma in genetic memory. We will use a *neuromorphic*[13] machine. After all, I am a co-creator of our shared reality. There is only one of me, so having thousands of genetic-memory healing machines would be great.

In the meantime, genetic-cloud healing is an opportunity to make heaven on earth for yourself and others who pursue the eternal goal of the integrated soul.

Peace be with you.
Piki te Ora
Piki te Kaha
Piki te Māramatanga

---

[13]   Neuromorphic intelligence: Artificial biological brain

Acknowledgements

I would like to acknowledge my Kaumatua Pereme Porter for preparing me to be who I really am – a matakite. He validated my spiritual reality behind the veil of everyday consciousness, and I want to honour his mana in our work together.

I would also like to acknowledge my aunties and uncles who have inspired me with insightful stories, a love of their culture, and the wonderful encouragement to be true to oneself.

A great big thank you to Alice, Florian, Scott, and Sue, who have contributed to this work, and many thanks to my spiritual community – both the seen and unseen.

Printed in the United States
By Bookmasters